Advance!

TIM CHALLIES

CRUCIFORM PRESS | JUNE 2018

CruciformPress
©CHALLIES

AUTHOR

Tim Challies is a Christian, a husband to Aileen, and a father to three teenage children. He is a co-founder of Cruciform Press and has written several books, including *Devoted, Visual Theology, Do More Better,* and *Sexual Detox.* He worships and serves as a pastor at Grace Fellowship Church in Toronto, Ontario and writes daily at www.challies.com.

 *We all know the feeling: every week, every month, every year it just seems that life keeps moving faster and faster. So we've taken our trademark length—books of about 100 pages—and added a set of resources that will make for even a quicker read. Cruciform Quick: a new line of booklets in the range of 40 to 60 pages each.*

ADVANCE!

Print / PDF ISBN: 978-1-941114-61-2
Mobipocket ISBN: 978-1-941114-62-9
ePub ISBN: 978-1-941114-63-6

Table of Contents

Patience, Priorities, Preparation

Nobody left a deeper or more indelible mark on history than Jesus of Nazareth. In his birth, life, death, and resurrection, he impacted lives, transformed nations, and changed the world. It is for good reason that we measure history with B.C. and A.D., with what came before the birth of Jesus and what came after. He forever stands at the very center of human existence.

Without a doubt, Jesus lived a life of great significance. But I wonder if you have ever considered this: Jesus had no lasting accomplishments before his 30s. We know this from the gospel accounts. After he died, four men wrote detailed biographies of his life: Matthew and John, who were his friends, and Mark and Luke, who were friends of his friends. These men spoke to his family and his followers, they interviewed people who knew him, they collected all the facts. And from all of their research, they mention just one detail about his teens and 20s: he was a carpenter, a normal man working a normal job.

Some early religious enthusiasts found this too hard to believe, so they embellished his story with tales of childhood miracles. The Gospel of Thomas, written more than 100 years after his death, fabricates stories of a young Jesus raising the dead and forming birds from clay to bring them to life. But we know this to be nonsense, an attempt to make sense of his normalcy, to excuse his early lack of accomplishments. In reality, one of the most remarkable facts about Jesus is how unremarkable he seemed in his teens and 20s.

Only Matthew and Luke record the facts surrounding Jesus' unusual birth, while Mark and John skip his childhood altogether and begin their narratives when he is already past 30. Only Luke records a glimpse of Jesus in his childhood, but then the record goes silent until he says, "Jesus, when he began his ministry, was about thirty years of age..." (Luke 3:23). Of all we know about the life and the deeds of Jesus the Messiah, almost everything takes place in a three-year window sometime after his 30th birthday.

This is not to say those silent years were wasted or that they served no purpose. To the contrary, the many years of anonymity were foundational to the few years of visibility. The Jesus of the three years of public ministry was formed during the 30 years of private obscurity. The 10 percent of his life that was carefully recorded cannot be separated from the 90 percent of his life that was not.

We can see something of these silent years in Luke's account. He gives us one glimpse of Jesus when he was 12, explaining that he willingly submitted to the care and oversight of his parents. Then he provides a brief summary of what Jesus was up to between 12 and 30: "And Jesus increased in wisdom and in stature and in favor with God and man" (Luke 2:52). In all these silent years, Jesus was advancing—advancing in obedience, wisdom, stature, and in favor with both God and man. In this way, we see that Jesus was actually full of accomplishments in his childhood, teens, and 20s. His accomplishments were accomplishments of character. His silent years laid the foundation of godly character that would enable and sustain him as he changed the world.

In this booklet I want to consider what Jesus accomplished in these years of silence, and I want to show how they were crucial to who he would become and what he would accomplish. From the life of Jesus, I want to encourage young

Christians to make the most of their teens and 20s by advancing first in accomplishments of character. Many young Christians have a noble desire to change the world and to do great things, but in most cases God intends to first change them and to do great things in their hearts and minds.

What follows will not be a call to lazy apathy but to deliberate priority. I'm going to call younger Christians to be patient, to establish right priorities, and to make your younger years a time of preparation. I'm going to plead with you to use these years not first to focus on outward accomplishments to shape the world, but inward achievements to shape your life. I want to ensure that as you advance in life, you advance first in character. In short, I want to call you to be like Jesus.

STUDY GUIDE

1. *How would you define a successful life?*

2. *What kinds of goals have you set for yourself for your remaining teenage years?*

3. *What kinds of outward accomplishments are you most proud of?*

4. *What inward achievements are you most proud of?*

5. *Do you measure your faith by your outward accomplishments or your inward achievements?*

CHAPTER 1

One Key Pursuit for Young Christians

Imagine for a moment that you have been charged with coming up with a life plan for the most important person in all of human history. The Messiah, the Son of God, will soon come to earth and will remain here for just over 30 years. He will be fully man, so you will need to plan accordingly, giving him time to grow from infancy to maturity, ensuring he has times of devotion to refresh his soul and of sleep to refresh his body. But he will also be fully God, so you will need to ensure he uses his perfect knowledge to explain the will of God and his perfect power to perform incredible miracles. It is up to you to plan the time between his birth and death.

If you were given such a task, you would most likely plan for Jesus to live as much of his life as possible in the public eye. You would want him to preach every sermon he possibly could, to perform every miracle, to tell every parable, to exorcise every demon. You would plan for him to grow up quickly so he could minister as publicly as possible for as long as possible. After all, you wouldn't want him to waste any of these precious years.

The Messiah, the Son of God, really did come to earth. But it fell to God—not you or me—to set the course for his life, and God planned it very differently. Jesus lived for around 33 years, but his entire public ministry fit into just the final three. He spent 90 percent of his life in obscurity and only ten percent in the public eye. For every one year that was recorded, there were ten that were not. God arranged the itinerary, and he chose to have Jesus spend 30 years in quiet preparation for his three years of public activity.

It should be both comforting and challenging to consider that the perfect, sinless Son of God celebrated his 30th birthday without any major accomplishments to his credit. To that point, his actions and achievements had been so unremarkable that his family and neighbors were flabbergasted when he at last began his public ministry. When he began to teach with authority and to perform great miracles, his neighbors sneered, "Isn't this the carpenter?" while his embarrassed family tried to hustle him away. Yet his silent years were not wasted years. His years between childhood and full adulthood were purposeful, and he used them to accomplish great things, even if they were invisible things. He lived these years so well that God himself would speak from the skies to commend him.

In this booklet we are discussing priorities for young Christians. The title and structure are drawn from the life of Jesus, from the words of one of his biographers who, in a sentence, summarizes Jesus' teens and 20s: "And Jesus increased in wisdom and in stature and in favor with God and man" (Luke 2:52). In this chapter, we are going to consider that simple word "increased" and how it challenges young Christians to one key pursuit.

ONE KEY PURSUIT

Embedded deep within the modern Western ethos is the idea that life never gets better than the teens and 20s. This trope is at the heart of a thousand Hollywood productions and cheesy pop songs. These are the years when you are most carefree, when expectation is low, when responsibility is minimal. These are the years when you are unrestrained by career, marriage, and children. According to this ethos, these years are best used to indulge in every desire, every freedom, and every fantasy, before you are at last forced to surrender to the inevitable and settle down into a hum-drum adulthood.

Many Christians have pushed back by teaching young believers to embrace these years for higher purposes and nobler pursuits. Rightly, they teach that the very activities the world advocates are the ones that will actually stain the years and squander them. They replace the low expectations of the world with the high expectations of God's Word. Well and good. Yet while this is a healthy reorientation, it may lead young Christians to believe that in order to make the most of their teens and 20s, they must have accomplishments that can be displayed—they must have written a book, or spoken at a conference, or founded a charity. They must have something that has earned accolades and garnered the praise and respect of others. At the very least, they may think the people who can display such accomplishments are the ones who have been most pleasing to God, the ones who are living best before him.

I have deep admiration for young Christians who want to make a difference in their church, in their community, and in their world. I would never wish to replace enthusiasm with apathy. However, I do need to raise the matter of priorities and insist that the most important priority for the teens and 20s is not external accomplishments but internal ones. The number one priority for young Christians is to advance in character. Life is not over at 30 but just beginning. The teens and 20s are not the time to live a whole life but to prepare for a whole life. In these years, young Christians need to prepare themselves for the rest of life by laying a foundation of godly character that will sustain them for the many years to come.

This does not mean that young Christians ought to substitute painstaking external accomplishments for more leisurely work on their character. Jesus' advancement in his character during his teens and 20s was far from easy. We know this because the word translated "increase" in Luke 2:52 carries the sense of advancing against obstacles and impediments. It is not the word for a leisurely stroll in the park but the word for blazing a trail in the woods. Jesus models the most strenuous, demanding kind of work for young Christians: the work of developing character.

Jesus himself needed time to prepare for public ministry. If Jesus needed time to prepare for his life's work, isn't it worth considering that perhaps you do, too? If even he was willing to put aside external accomplishments to focus first on internal achievements, shouldn't you be willing to do the same? Even Jesus had to be before he could do, to develop his character before he could minister effectively. In the end, Jesus used 90 percent of his life in preparation! Yet these years of preparation did not frustrate God or thwart his purposes. Rather, they pleased God and fulfilled his purposes.

WELL PLEASED

Jesus' public ministry began with his baptism. His cousin John had gone "into all the region around the Jordan, proclaiming a baptism of repentance for the forgiveness of sins" (Luke 3:3). He warned people to turn away from their sin and to prepare themselves for the coming of the Messiah. Crowds were flocking to John to hear his message and to respond with repentance, confession, and baptism. So many came that Matthew says that "Jerusalem and all Judea and all the region about the Jordan were going out to him" (Matthew 3:5). Genuine revival was stirring.

Then one day Jesus shows up. When he is around 30, he

comes from Galilee to the Jordan and asks John to baptize him just like everyone else. John knows Jesus' true identity and is shocked and offended by the very notion of baptizing him. "John would have prevented him, saying, 'I need to be baptized by you, and do you come to me?'" (Matthew 3:14). But Jesus insists, saying, "Let it be so now, for thus it is fitting for us to fulfill all righteousness" (verse 15). John consents and lowers his cousin into the water.

As Jesus emerges from the waters of the Jordan River, something remarkable happens. "The heavens were opened, and the Holy Spirit descended on him in bodily form, like a dove; and a voice came from heaven, 'You are my beloved Son; with you I am well pleased'" (Luke 3:21-22). God the Father tells God the Son of his delight in him, of his satisfaction in the life he has lived. "I take pleasure in you. I approve of who you are. I am satisfied in all you have accomplished."

What has Jesus accomplished? As far as we know, up until this point, Jesus has a one-line resume: carpenter. He has not yet preached his first sermon, told his first parable, exorcised his first demon, or performed his first miracle. He has no medals to hang around his neck, no awards to pin on his chest, no accolades to trim from the local newspaper and carefully glue into his scrapbook.

The one thing he does have to his credit is character. He has carefully, deliberately, substantially advanced in character. And that is enough. It is more than enough for God, his Father. He has done the very thing God has called him to do for 30 years. He has advanced in obedience, in wisdom, in stature, and in favor with God and man. He has prepared himself in obscurity for a ministry he will fulfill with great publicity. He has obeyed God. He is prepared for what God has for him.

Young Christian, look to Jesus and see that the most important advances you can make in your teens and 20s are advances in character. It is in these years that you will lay a foundation of godly character capable of guiding and sustaining you for a lifetime. Your one key pursuit for your teens and 20s must be to advance. Follow after your Savior and advance in godly character, advance in obedience, advance in wisdom, advance in favor with God and man.

STUDY GUIDE

1. *How have you bought into worldly ideas about your adolescence? These worldly ideas can vary from being justified in wasting your years with fun and pleasure or perhaps being known for an incredible accomplishment.*

2. *Do you see how it affects your attitudes towards responsibility and your mindset on adulthood? Do you notice how it affects the goals and plans you set for yourself?*

3. *How do you see yourself making a difference in your family, in your friendships, school, church, and community?*

4. *Are you preparing yourself for adulthood? How?*

CHAPTER 2

Advance in Submission

Why was Jesus born into the world as a baby instead of arriving as a fully-grown man? Did he really have to endure infancy with its helplessness, childhood with its ignorance, those teenage years with their awkwardness? Why didn't he just arrive at 30, bang out his mission in three short years, and then make a quick escape from this sin-stained world?

The author of the letter to the Hebrews answers our questions: "Although he was a son, he learned obedience through what he suffered. And being made perfect, he became the source of eternal salvation to all who obey him" (Hebrews 5:8-9). To complete his mission, the Son of God had to live a complete life as a man. He had to be a baby, he had to be a toddler, he had to be a child, a tween, a teen, a young adult, and a grown man. He had to face and endure the temptations that come with every one of life's stages. He had to be tempted as a toddler to defy his parents, as a teen to retaliate against sinful brothers and sisters, as an adult to be quick-tempered and sharp-tongued. He was tempted in every way we are, yet he never sinned (Hebrews 4:15).

But he did not only need to avoid temptation; he also needed to express perfect obedience. He had to perfectly avoid the sins of each of the 10 commandments and also model complete adherence to them. He had to avoid worship of all other gods, and he also had to worship the true and living God. He had to avoid taking God's name in vain, and he also had to always speak well of the Father. He had to refrain from murdering anyone, and he also had to express love to every person all of the time. God's commandments are not just sins to avoid but also righteousness to obey. In all of history, only Christ has perfectly avoided all sin and perfectly achieved all righteousness, and this is why he can be our Savior.

Among these 10 commandments, there is one that stands out as especially unusual for this God-man to obey: "Honor your father and your mother, that your days may be long in the land that the LORD your God is giving you" (Exodus 20:12). For Jesus to live a perfect life and to perfectly obey God's law, he would have to honor parents. He who had existed from eternity would have to obey mortal beings. He who had created all things would have to honor those he had brought into existence. He, the perfect Son of God, would have to submit to an imperfect mother and father. To be a suitable Savior, he would need to willingly subject himself to Mary and Joseph.

As we continue our look at the silent years between Jesus' childhood and public ministry, we first encounter his submission. Luke comments on these 18 years when he says, "And he went down with them and came to Nazareth and was submissive to them" (Luke 2:51). Jesus used his teens and 20s to advance in submission. As we will see, this obedient submission was essential to the other advances Luke highlights—advances in wisdom, stature, and favor. From Jesus we learn that young Christians who wish to advance in those other noble qualities must first advance in submission.

HE WAS SUBMISSIVE TO THEM

Children are naturally rebellious. Even as tiny infants they begin to express discontent with their parents, and already as toddlers they begin to defy every form of authority. Mary and Joseph eventually had a large family, and they would have done their utmost to raise their children in the discipline and instruction of the Lord. They would have told their children to honor their mother and father, they would have disciplined them for their defiance, they would have pleaded with them for obedience. All of them but one, that is. Each of Mary's other children were daughters or sons of Joseph, but Jesus was the Son of God. Because he was conceived by the Holy Spirit, he had no sin and no sinful desire to defy his parents.

Jesus spent his childhood, his teens, and his 20s in submission to his parents. Never once did he sinfully defy them. Never once did he rebel against their authority. Never once did he talk back in spite. To the contrary, he only ever joyfully and voluntarily submitted to them. He willingly put himself under their leadership, under their direction, and under their authority.

His submission was the kind of submission God calls for in the fifth commandment. This is a submission that takes the form of obedience and honor. Jesus submitted by obeying his parents and honoring his parents.

OBEDIENCE

The Bible has much to say about the relationship of children to their parents, but we can distill it to something like this: All children are to honor their parents; young children are to obey their parents. Childhood obedience is the training ground for mature honor. This why the commandment given to Moses is more broad: "Honor your father and your mother..." (Exodus 20:12). But when Paul addresses young children, he says, "Children, obey your parents in the Lord, for this is right" (Ephesians 6:1). All children owe their parents lifelong honor, while young children also owe their parents joyful obedience.

Young children are to obey their parents because children

need to be trained. Children enter the world rebellious and in need of moral guidance, unknowledgeable and in need of intellectual guidance, graceless and in need of social guidance. Parents are right to expect and demand obedience of their young children as they teach and train them in virtue.

Because Jesus was fully human, he was dependent upon his parents like any other child. His parents had wisdom and knowledge from the world that he did not have, so it was their responsibility to train him, and it was his responsibility to obey them. So we can imagine that Jesus listened carefully and obeyed them as they told him to sit still at the table, to make eye contact with grown ups, to behave respectfully in the temple. He would have obeyed them when they told him to run an errand, to scrub the dishes, to sweep the wood shop. He obeyed them by always "doing it now, doing it right, and doing it with a happy heart." For as long as Jesus was under the authority of his parents, he obeyed his parents.

You, too, must obey your parents as long as you remain under their authority. If Jesus could admit his lack of wisdom and knowledge and learn from his mother and father, so can you. If the perfect Son of God needed the guidance of imperfect parents, so do you. If he joyfully obeyed them, you can joyfully obey your parents. The only time you can rightly disobey them is when they require something of you that God forbids. Otherwise, you need to advance in character by advancing in obedience. You need to acknowledge that submission to God is displayed first in submission to your parents.

HONOR

Jesus obeyed his parents, and he also honored them. As he aged and gained greater independence, his childhood obedience gave way to mature honor. His obedience to his parents developed his character to the point where he no longer needed as much direct guidance. It was no longer necessary or even fitting for him to obey. This was a good and natural progression. But until his dying day, it would remain necessary and fitting for him to show honor.

The word we translate as "honor" refers to weight or significance and indicates that we are to assign great worth to our parents and great importance to our relationship with them. We are to speak well of them, to express gratitude to them, and to treat them with kindness and dignity. Honor is an inward attitude that is displayed in outward actions. As our parents age, we are to honor them by caring for them and even providing for them. We see Jesus doing this very thing as he was nailed to the cross. "When Jesus saw his mother and the disciple whom he loved standing nearby, he said to his mother, 'Woman, behold, your son!' Then he said to the disciple, 'Behold, your mother!' And from that hour the disciple took her to his own home" (John 19:26-27). In his last hours, Jesus expressed honor to his mother by ensuring she would be cared for into her old age.

Once again, if Jesus had to show honor to his parents, so do you. And if Jesus could show honor to his parents, so can you. Your parents are imperfect and at times unjust. Your parents may have unrealistic expectations or make unfair demands. Yet you owe them a lifelong debt of honor and, like Jesus, need to advance in character by advancing in honor.

THE SUBMISSIVE SAVIOR

For nearly 18 years, Jesus was lost to history. Yet in these 18 years, he made the advances that would shape his character and prepare him for his mission. Years that may look wasted were actually put to the most important use. Jesus committed these years to submitting to his parents, to advancing in obedience and honor.

This submission was crucial to the other advances he made. Had Jesus spent these years in rebellion against his parents, he could not have advanced in wisdom, in stature, or in favor with God and man. It was within the context of a family—this family—that God would shape him. It was by submitting to parents—these parents—that God would fit him to ministry. The God who had planned the events of his later life had equally planned the context for his childhood, his teens, and his 20s. By submitting to his parents, he was preparing to submit to the will of God to such an extent that he even "humbled himself by becoming obedient to the point of death, even death on a cross" (Philippians 2:8).

Young Christian, you are also commanded to heed the fifth commandment. How can you expect to obey God through great accomplishments later in life if you will not obey God in this simple command now? While you remain under the authority of your parents, you owe them obedience. When you have grown beyond their authority, you owe them honor. As you honor and obey your parents, you are honoring and obeying God. It is in this context of joyful submission to God's will that you can expect to advance in the other qualities that marked the life of young Jesus—wisdom, stature, and favor before God and man. As Jesus advanced in submission to his earthly parents and heavenly Father, he was preparing himself for the life God had for him. By advancing in submission to your earthly parents and your heavenly Father, you too are preparing yourself for all God wants to complete in you and through you.

STUDY GUIDE

1. *In what ways have you submitted to your parents today, this week, this month?*

2. *How have you rebelled towards your parents today, this week, this month?*

3. *Do you submit to your parents out of joy or duty?*

4. *What are creative ways in which you can show your parents honor? How will you plan and execute that in the coming days?*

5. *Even if you have a difficult or complicated relationship with your parents, reflect on ways in which you have benefited from them. How can you show your gratitude for these things?*

CHAPTER 3

Advance in Wisdom

Since 2004, Dove has been promoting their products with the Real Beauty campaign. Several years ago, they released a video titled "Real Beauty Sketches," and it quickly went viral. In this video, they had a number of women describe themselves to a hidden forensic sketch artist. He listened to them and created a drawing based on their description of their physical characteristics. Then the subject left the room, and a second person entered who had met the woman only the day before. This person was also asked to describe her while the artist created a second sketch. Not surprisingly, this second drawing was not only a more accurate depiction of the subject but also a far more attractive one. Each of the women was deeply moved to learn that others had assessed her more accurately and more favorably than she had assessed herself. It was a clever video that made its point well.

But I can't help but wonder if in the end it actually made much of a difference in the lives of these women. After all, it is one thing to gain another person's assessment of ourselves but a very different thing to believe it. In fact, one of the hardest things to do is believe what other people say about us, especially when it contradicts our self-assessment. Sometimes we have too low a view of ourselves, as was the case in the Dove commercial. But because of our indwelling sin, we also can have too high a view of ourselves. We are sometimes too close to ourselves to see clearly, too proud to see ourselves as we really are.

In this chapter you will hear an important assessment of yourself and your character. It will not be easy to believe because the results will not be pretty. You will be tempted to doubt them, to deny them, or to excuse them away. But as others often have a better view of ourselves than we do, the Bible gives us the most accurate view of ourselves, allowing us to advance our character from a sober understanding of our position.

ADVANCE IN WISDOM

I am one of those people who just wants to be told it like it is. Don't dress it up, don't beat around the bush, and don't be too concerned with offending me. Whatever you do, don't try to be cute by sandwiching a heavy rebuke between two trite encouragements. Please, just tell me the truth, and I'll do my best to deal with it.

Maybe that's part of what first drew me to the Bible. The Bible is blunt. It never shies away from tough or uncomfortable truths. Instead, it just lays them on us and asks, "So, what do you plan to do about it?" The Bible's blunt truth you need to grapple with right now is this: You are foolish. At least, you are not as wise as you were created to be, as you ought to be, and as you someday will be. This lack of wisdom is partly the product of your natural humanity and partly the product of your unnatural depravity. In both cases, you are responsible before God to acknowledge it and address it.

Do you need proof of your lack of wisdom? Just read the book of Proverbs. Solomon wrote this book for young people with the premise that they are foolish and in desperate need of wisdom. He begins with his statement of purpose: "To know wisdom and instruction, to understand words of insight, to receive instruction in wise dealing, in righteousness, justice, and equity; to give prudence to the simple, knowledge and discretion to the youth" (1:2-4). Implicit in the necessity of obtaining wisdom, insight, and instruction is the acknowledgment that you don't already have it. To succeed in life, you will need prudence, knowledge, and discretion that you do not yet have. These attributes come with age and effort.

In Proverbs we see concerned parents pleading with their children to become wise: "Hear, my son, your father's instruction, and forsake not your mother's teaching, for they are a graceful garland for your head and pendants for your neck" (1:8-9). We see Wisdom personified and crying out to people just like you: "How long, O simple ones, will you love being simple? How long will scoffers delight in their scoffing and fools hate knowledge? If you turn at my reproof, behold, I will pour out my spirit to you; I will make my words known to you" (1:22-23). We read of the tremendous blessings available to the wise: "Blessed is the one who finds wisdom, and the one who gets understanding, for the gain from her is better than gain from silver and her profit better than gold. She is more precious than jewels, and nothing you desire can compare with her" (3:13-15). We read of the ugly woes promised to those who forsake wisdom: "Toward the scorners [God] is scornful, but to the humble he gives favor. The wise will inherit honor, but fools get disgrace" (3:34-35). From the first to the last chapter of Proverbs, Solomon pleads with young people to turn away from the path of foolishness and to walk on the path of wisdom. The book of Proverbs is one solid proof that you are foolish and need wisdom.

A second proof comes when Luke summarizes Jesus' life between childhood and the start of his public ministry at around age 30. He tells us that Jesus "increased in wisdom and in stature and in favor with God and man" (Luke 2:52). Even Jesus, who was God, had to advance in wisdom because he was a man. In his divine nature, Jesus had complete knowledge and complete wisdom; in his human nature he had no more knowledge and no more wisdom than any other child. If the young Jesus needed to advance in wisdom, surely you do, too.

How did Jesus advance in such wisdom? First, he submitted to his parents in obedience and honor, since he, like any other child, was deeply dependent upon their wisdom to navigate his early life. They were his first and most important teachers as they undoubtedly heeded God's command to parents: "You shall teach [God's words] diligently to your children, and shall talk of them when you sit in your house, and when you walk by the way, and when you lie down, and when you rise" (Deuteronomy 6:7). Second, from the one glimpse we get of the boy Jesus, we also see how he learned from religious authorities. On that occasion, he was "sitting among the teachers, listening to them and asking them questions" (Luke 2:46). He sought out teachers, he put himself under their authority, he asked questions to clarify what he did not understand, and he used his growing wisdom to express what he knew.

Jesus advanced in wisdom. As his followers, we are called to advance in wisdom as he did, to move out of the immaturity of childhood into the maturity that wisdom brings. But as sinners, our advancement in wisdom will be marred by foolishness and sin—downfalls that Jesus never experienced as the sinless Son of God.

GROWING WISE LIKE JESUS

As an infant, Jesus knew only what infants know, which is not very much. He had to learn the most basic skills—standing, talking, controlling his bodily functions. As a child, Jesus behaved like any other child—he explored his environment, he learned social skills, he discovered facts about God, he grew in his understanding of the world. At some point, he even came to grasp his own identity as the long-awaited Messiah and to consciously embrace the mission God had assigned to him. Like all of us, he went through a long process of maturation in which he advanced in wisdom. Perhaps we can define that wisdom in three categories: knowledge, reason, and emotion.

As Jesus matured, he accumulated knowledge. By formal teaching, informal observation, and diligent memorization, he learned about himself, his family, his people, his nation, and his world. Added to these was knowledge about God and the Scriptures, about language, math, geography, and every other discipline. Then there was all that his father taught him about carpentry, the profession that would occupy him for most of his life. He began infancy with a mind that was an empty slate and, like all of us, gave his younger years to gaining knowledge.

As Jesus matured, he also learned to reason. He learned the difference between a compelling line of argumentation and a trite one. He learned to ask leading questions that would draw people out and to answer questions in a way that would stimulate further conversation. He learned to teach effectively through extended sermons and simple parables. The Jesus who later wowed great crowds and confounded furious Pharisees is the Jesus whose mind was formed and trained in childhood and young adulthood. It was in these years that he learned the reasoning skills that would forever mark him as history's greatest teacher.

Finally, as Jesus matured, he learned to govern his emotions and to put them to the best use. Like any other little boy, he once would have laughed at things that weren't actually funny and cried at things that were hardly reasons for great grief. Like all teenagers, he would have been prone to sudden changes in mood. But he learned to control his emotions and to use them well. This Jesus would later put his emotions to effective use in angrily driving money changers out of the temple, compassionately weeping over Jerusalem, and hilariously poking fun at the kind of people who fret over a speck in another person's eye while ignoring the giant log protruding from their own.

In these silent years, Jesus advanced in wisdom. He learned how to best apply what he learned to life. He accumulated knowledge and the understanding of how to effectively teach that knowledge to others. He mastered his emotions so he could rejoice with those who rejoice and grieve with those who grieve. Because his mind was unhindered by sin, it rose to the highest heights possible for a human mind. In these years, he prepared himself for who he would become and for what he would accomplish.

In that way, Jesus provides an example of how you can put your teens and 20s to good use. Of primary importance is learning wisdom from parents and pastors. God calls you to submit to the leadership of your parents when you are young, to obey them in all they ask of you. But whether you are young or old, you should equally honor their wisdom by speaking to them and deliberately learning from the wisdom they have accumulated over many years. At the same time, learn wisdom from your pastors. Commit to your local church as the place you will serve, worship, and learn. Place yourself under the authority of the leadership there and learn God's wisdom as they teach it in their words and display it in their lives.

GROWING WISE AS SINNERS

By virtue of his natural humanity, Jesus lacked wisdom and had much to learn, just like you. Yet Jesus was morally perfect, unlike you. Because he was the Son of God, he was unstained by sin and unmarred by moral foolishness. Jesus was born holy, but you need to become holy. You are not only battling immaturity in your advancement in wisdom but also foolishness.

When the Bible describes human beings as "fools," it sometimes refers to a simple lack of knowledge. Other times, though, it refers to something far more insidious—the natural atheism that inhabits the hearts of all who are born sinful. This is the kind of person David refers to in Psalm 14:1: "The fool says in his heart, 'There is no God.'" Foolish people rebel against God and declare independence from God. Of all the human beings who have ever lived, only Jesus has ever been entirely free of this kind of foolishness. Only he was completely unstained by sin from conception to death.

What was true of David is true of you: "I was brought forth in iniquity, and in sin did my mother conceive me" (Psalm 51:5). You were sinful from the moment of your conception, rebellious from before you drew your first breath. You were a fool in that deepest, darkest sense.

Yet you have put your faith in Jesus Christ and been indwelt by the Holy Spirit. You have been saved by his grace and forgiven for every sin. You're a Christian and long to live like one. The great challenge that will consume the rest of your life is to become who you are in Christ—to put to death all the sin that remains within and to come alive to the righteousness given to you by Christ. You will battle to your dying day to stop behaving foolishly in rebellion to God and to instead live wisely in submission to God.

Many young people waste their teens and 20s by committing these precious years to sin and foolish indulgence. Young Christian, you can put these years to the best use by making great strides in holiness. You can commit your teen years to destroying foolishness and growing in wisdom. You can commit your 20s to living wisely instead of foolishly. You can commit them all to living in holy ways instead of depraved ways. As you do that, you will lay a foundation of wise thinking and wise living that serve you well for the rest of your life.

CONCLUSION

"The beginning of wisdom is this," says Solomon. "Get wisdom, and whatever you get, get insight" (Proverbs 4:7). Jesus knew and heeded these words. He acknowledged his lack of wisdom, and he joyfully submitted to those called to teach and train him. As he prepared to live out his God-given purpose, he prepared his mind by training it to be wise. Just as he committed his teens and his 20s to this noble pursuit, so you ought to devote yourself to advancing in wisdom.

STUDY GUIDE

1. *Are you advancing in the following areas of wisdom?*

    • **Knowledge.** *Are you growing in knowledge about the world? Are you growing in knowledge about the Bible? Do you take learning seriously?*

    • **Reason.** *Are you advancing your ability to reason tough arguments? Do you think critically about the worldview expressed by your teachers and your friends? Do you ask questions when the sermon you listen to is unclear to you, or because you simply want to make more sense of it?*

    • **Emotion.** *Would you consider yourself to be full of self-control? Do you have outbursts of anger? Do you laugh at things that are inappropriate? Are you a sarcastic person? Are your comments appropriate and commendable?*

2. *Who do you turn to when you need wisdom?*

3. *Do you feel the freedom to speak to your pastors when you are in need of their wisdom?*

4. *Are you someone younger Christians can turn to for wisdom and advice? Why or why not?*

CHAPTER 4

Advance in Stature

How big is God? This is the kind of question most children ask at one time or another. They know that they are weak and that God is strong, they know that they are tiny and that the universe is immense, and so they naturally wonder, "Just how big is this God, anyway?" And in some way, their parents explain that God is spiritual, not physical, infinite, not limited, with no form and therefore no size. God is neither big nor small—he is everywhere at all times.

But then we open the New Testament and read words like these: "For unto you is born this day in the city of David a Savior, who is Christ the Lord. And this will be a sign for you: you will find a baby wrapped in swaddling cloths and lying in a manger" (Luke 2:11-12).

How big is God? About 20 inches and seven pounds. Then a month later, 22 inches and nine pounds. And a year after that, 30 inches and 20 pounds. This is the wonder of the incarnation of Jesus, the second person of the Trinity confining himself to a human body. Charles Wesley marveled at this in one of his lesser-known hymns: "Our God contracted to a span / incomprehensibly made Man." The eternal Word took on the tiny form of a newborn, the omnipotent creator the helpless body of a baby, the omniscient God the simple mind of an infant.

As Jesus grew from a child to an adult, his biographer Luke reports that in his teens and 20s, "Jesus increased in wisdom and in *stature* and in favor with God and man" (Luke 2:52). Like any other human being, he grew in stature, in physical height and weight. Over the years, his childish body slowly gave way to an adult body. Along the way, he would have endured the clumsiness that follows childhood growth spurts and the endless appetite that arrives with the teenage years. He would have gone through puberty and its sexual maturing, developing his first facial hair, outgrowing his clothes and passing them down to his brothers. He did all the things normal people do as they advance from childhood to manhood.

This alone is a marvel: that God grew. Yet as he grew in physical stature, he experienced another kind of growth that would prove equally important, that would help him develop into full maturity. Hand in hand with his physical advance came steady spiritual advance. Jesus' body grew in all holiness. Of particular relevance to young adults is this: As he advanced out of childhood into manhood, he renounced the lust that so often grips those whose bodies are developing. From the beginning of his earthly life and through his teens and 20s, Jesus shows us how to offer our bodies as a living sacrifice, refusing to give in to sexual temptation. In all this, he was preparing for his ultimate offering to God, the sacrifice of his body on the cross.

As we continue through this booklet, we need to consider your teens and 20s as a time to advance in stature. This will include the development of your body and the arrival of its peak strength. Of even greater importance, though, this will include the development of your soul. As you develop and establish your physical stature, you must also develop and establish your spiritual stature, standing firm in sexual purity and renouncing youthful lust.

PHYSICAL STATURE

Since the church's earliest days, many who have claimed the name "Christian" have downplayed the body in favor of the soul. The soul is good, they say, and the body bad, so that this good soul needs to be liberated from this bad body. The Bible teaches something very different. It teaches that God made the human body as the ideal dwelling place for the human soul. The body was made to be good just as the soul was made to be good. And as if to prove its goodness, God the Son took up permanent residence in the human body. Today he lives and reigns as the God who is man.

You live within a body that was created by God. In fact, this body was specially created for you so you could use it to glorify God. When David considered this, he marveled. "For you formed my inward parts; you knitted me together in my mother's womb. I praise you, for I am fearfully and wonderfully made. Wonderful are your works; my soul knows it very well" (Psalm 139:13-14). Of all that God created, humans are the greatest and most glorious, for human beings alone are created in the image of God and human beings alone are the dwelling place for God.

As you grow in physical stature, you gain the responsibility to understand the purpose of your body and the necessity of using it for the best and highest purposes. Your body is not worthless packaging to use and discard but a valuable creation to nurture and protect. God tells you to take responsibility for your body by presenting it to him, then stewarding, nurturing, employing, and guarding it. Let's look at each of these in turn.

You need to present your body. In his letter to the church at Rome, Paul says, "I appeal to you therefore, brothers, by the mercies of God, to present your bodies as a living sacrifice, holy and acceptable to God, which is your spiritual worship" (Romans 12:1). We are whole people, bodies and souls knit carefully together. We are to surrender to God all that we are, holding nothing back. Even our bodies belong to God and are to be used for the purposes of God. Thus, God calls us to surrender our bodies to him, to dedicate them to his service, to commit them to his purposes.

You need to steward your body. As you surrender your body, you acknowledge that it does not belong to you but to God. He made it and he owns it, but he has given it to you to manage. This is what we call "stewardship," managing something on behalf of someone else. Just as you are responsible to faithfully steward your time and money, you are responsible before God to faithfully steward the body he has assigned to you. You are to use your body wisely, to put your body to use in ways that bring glory to God. After all, "You are not your own, for you were bought with a price. So glorify God in your body" (1 Corinthians 6:19-20).

You need to nurture your body. There is an inseparable unity between body, mind, and soul. When we neglect our bodies, we often find our souls heavy and our minds dark. But when we care for our bodies, we find our souls cheerful and our minds enlightened. We see some of this in John's prayer for his friend Gaius: "Beloved, I pray that all may go well with you and that you may be in good health, as it goes well with your soul" (3 John 2). For Gaius to be as active and effective as possible in God's work, he must have a healthy body and a healthy soul. If you wish to tend to your soul and mind, you must nurture your body. To honor God in all that you are, you must eat well, exercise frequently, and rest regularly.

You need to employ your body. Inner godliness is to be displayed in outward acts of kindness. James shows the unity of faith and works in this illustration: "If a brother or sister is poorly clothed and lacking in daily food, and one of you says to them, 'Go in peace, be warmed and filled,' without giving them the things needed for the body, what good is that? So also faith by itself, if it does not have works, is dead" (James 2:15-17). The love of God in your heart is to be displayed by the works of your hands. Young people are at their physical peak and bear a double responsibility to use that strength for the good of others. "The glory of young men is their strength," says Solomon, "but the splendor of old men is their gray hair" (Proverbs 20:29). Later in life you can dazzle people with your wisdom, but for now you can best serve them with your strength.

The human body is holy, created by God for the glory of God. An important part of growing in physical stature is growing into an awareness of what the body is for and how to best use it. This is the time in life to form healthy patterns of living, eating, exercising, working, and resting. By devoting your body to God and nurturing it for its maximum performance, you are preparing yourself for a life of good works for the glory of God.

SPIRITUAL STATURE

Just as the body can be treated well to do good things, it can also be treated poorly to do evil things. Along with the development of our bodies in our teens and 20s comes the temptation to give our bodies to sexual sin instead of God. An essential component of advancing like Jesus is guarding our bodies against sexual sin as we physically grow.

One of the attributes of every human being is sexuality. We were created by God to be sexual beings. By virtue of our humanity we have sexual organs, sexual ability, and sexual desire. Having created us with this sexual capacity, God created marriage as the appropriate context in which to express it, then commanded us to use that context to "be fruitful and multiply and fill the earth and subdue it" (Genesis 1:28). God gave us all we need to enjoy and employ the precious gift of sex.

Because Jesus was fully human, he was a sexual being with sexual organs, sexual ability, and sexual desire. He was not an androgynous or asexual being, but a normal human being with testosterone flowing through his veins. In his teens he, like any other person, would have grown in sexual desire.

Because Jesus was fully human, he probably experienced sexual temptation. After all, the Bible insists he "in every respect has been tempted as we are, yet without sin" (Hebrews 4:15). Just as Satan tempted Jesus in the wilderness to break the first commandment ("You shall have no other gods before me"), he may at other times have tempted him to break the seventh commandment ("You shall not commit adultery"). Yet Jesus "committed no sin, neither was deceit found in his mouth" (1 Peter 2:22). He endured these temptations without any sinful thoughts, deeds, or even desires.

There are several important lessons young Christians can learn from Jesus.

First, Jesus was fully human and faced every temptation that comes with being a warm-blooded human. Yet he passed through his teens and 20s without ever succumbing to sexual sin. He did not cheat and borrow from his "godness" to do this, but rather he faced and overcame temptation *as a man*. As a man, he lived a perfectly holy life, content in his chastity.

Second, Jesus endured temptation and lived in perfect purity because he was dependent on the Holy Spirit. Jesus' success offers us tremendous comfort, "for because he himself has suffered when tempted, he is able to help those who are being tempted" (Hebrews 2:18). As you face inevitable onslaughts of sexual desire or opportunity, you can turn to him for both sympathy and assistance, for the very Spirit who lived within him now lives within us. The Spirit not only comforts us but also warns us of sin and works in us to overcome it (1 Thessalonians 4:8).

Third, Jesus demonstrates that a meaningful and fulfilling life is not dependent upon sexual fulfillment. Rather, we can have fulfillment without ever having sex. After all, no one has ever lived a better life than Jesus, yet he lived and died a virgin. His perfect model of a God-honoring life did not include sex or marriage.

By living a life free from sexual expression, Jesus demonstrates that you can be complete and fulfilled without sexual experience and sexual fulfillment. By living a life free from sexual sin, Jesus shows how you also can live your teens and 20s and even the rest of your life without ever succumbing to sexual impurity. How can you be sure? Because you are indwelt by the same Spirit who filled Jesus. The power that was available to him to resist temptation and motivate holiness is available to you if only you will take hold of it.

Young Christian, if you long to advance as Jesus advanced, you must also guard yourself against sexual sin and pursue purity with all your heart. Just as you present your body to God, present your sexuality to God, resolving to only express sexuality in holiness within the context of marriage. Just as you are called to steward your body, you must also steward your sexuality, receiving sex as a gift from God that must be used within the design of God. Just as you must nurture your body, nurture your sexuality by making investments of purity now that will reap benefits later within marriage and eternity.

Young Christian, if you have already failed, if you have already given your body to lust instead of God, there is hope! The Jesus who perfectly models sexual purity is the same Jesus who sacrificially died for your sexual impurity. Turn to him, receive his forgiveness, and commit yourself again to the Savior who died on your behalf.

CONCLUSION

Jesus passed through his teens and 20s in a sexually charged culture. He was surrounded by sin and depravity, a witness to every kind of enticement. Yet he resisted all temptation, and he achieved all righteousness. As he grew in physical stature, he also grew in spiritual stature by abstaining from sexual immorality and controlling his body in holiness and honor. He fully depended upon God and did all things to the glory of God. He shows the way to surrender our bodies to God, he shows the way to devote our sexuality to God, he shows the way to joy, to fullness of life.

STUDY GUIDE

1. *What are some of the ways you care for your body? What are some of the ways you don't?*

2. *Do you prioritize rest? Honestly, do you get the rest you need to function at your highest level?*

3. *How do you use your strength for the good of others? Spend some time thinking about how you can use your youthful energy and strength to bless others.*

4. *How are you guarding yourself against sexual sin?*

   • *Have you repented for falling into temptation to lustful thoughts or viewing pornography? Do you keep yourself accountable to someone when you fall into temptation? The Bible is clear that we must flee temptation towards sexual sin. How will you overcome temptation?*

5. *It is easy to become discouraged when we fall into the same temptations time and time again. But the Bible provides us with so much hope! Turn to Christ and receive his forgiveness. Continue to commit your way to him.*

CHAPTER 5

Advance in Favor

When I was in my early 20s, one of my friends had a sudden experience of spiritual growth and enthusiasm. Suddenly, he had a new fervor for the Lord and a fresh desire to serve him. He began using new words and imaginative phrases to describe his relationship with God and his longing to live for his glory. One of these was "audience of One." "I don't care what other people think of me," he said. "I'm just going to live before an audience of One."

I quickly learned what he meant. He was determined not to be concerned with what people thought of him but to instead seek out and live the will of God, no matter the cost. In these days of enthusiasm, only God's opinion mattered to him. I lost touch with my friend soon after his big commitment, so I never learned how well he succeeded. I knew his intentions were sincere, but as I considered his catchphrase, I came to wonder whether he had actually mastered the Bible's emphasis on life in this world.

Are we to live before an audience of One? Yes and no. Nothing is more important than knowing God's will, living it out, and enjoying his approval. The Bible has much to say about living lives that are pleasing to God. Yet the Bible also has much to say about living lives that receive the approval of man. Often these two go hand-in-hand, and we see this connection in the life of Jesus. Luke tells us that in his teens and 20s, "Jesus increased in wisdom and in stature and in favor with God and man" (Luke 2:52).

In this booklet we have already seen how the young Jesus advanced in submission, in wisdom, and in stature. As he advanced in those noble character traits and the actions they motivated, he enjoyed the favor of both God and man. We cannot end until we have taken a close look at this advance in favor and applied it to the life of all young Christians.

ADVANCE IN FAVOR

As a society, we give a lot of attention to approval. We love to analyze and quantify it, especially in the political realm. Endless polls and surveys ask us to rank and rate our politicians. We then display and discuss these approval ratings through numbers, graphs, and charts. For politicians to rule by the assent of the people, they must enjoy the approval of the people, so they rely on such polls to evaluate their accomplishments and to plot their future plans. Political careers are created and broken on the backs of the pollsters. Approval can be a reasonable desire or an insatiable idol.

As Jesus grew in wisdom and stature, he enjoyed the approval of both God and man. In the opening days of his ministry, God the Father cracked open the skies to assure him, "You are my beloved Son; with you I am well pleased" (Luke 3:22). Meanwhile, Jesus' first sermons at the synagogues met the approval of the townsfolk so that, "all spoke well of him and marveled at the gracious words that were coming from his mouth" (Luke 4:22). Though some scoffed at him, all of them recognized that he was "teaching them as one who had authority" (Matthew 7:29). The Son of God and man was in the favor of God and man.

It should not surprise us that he was regarded so favorably. Centuries earlier, King Solomon had called young people to pursue wisdom and attempted to motivate them with the result: "My son, do not forget my teaching, but let your heart keep my commandments... So you will find favor and good success in the sight of God and man" (Proverbs 3:1, 4). Jesus walked on that path of wisdom and gained the promised result—the favor of God and of people. Had he been a foolish, immature rebel, he would have deserved only pity and condemnation. But he committed his teens and 20s to obedience, wisdom, and godly living, and gained the fitting reward.

God offers that same reward to you. Just as Jesus advanced in the favor of God and man, so can you. So *should* you. But the order must be right. Where men's approval is flawed and fading, God's is perfect and unchanging. Therefore, we must live first for him. "For am I now seeking the approval of man, or of God? Or am I trying to please man? If I were still trying to please man, I would not be a servant of Christ" (Galatians 1:10). There may be times you can have the approval of only one, because gaining the favor of God will cost the favor of man. For this reason we will look first at how and why you must pursue the favor of God above all else.

PURSUE THE FAVOR OF GOD

You have the favor of God. God not only loves you, but the gospel also assures you that he approves of you. You have been saved by the grace of God, which means you have the full acceptance of God. There is nothing you can accomplish to make God approve of you more and no sin you can commit to make God approve of you less. This complete and unchanging approval is yours by virtue of what Christ accomplished on your behalf.

All of this is true in an ultimate sense. Yet there is also a sense in which it is possible for God to be more or less pleased with you. Perhaps we can best explain this by the familiar analogy of a child and his parents. A child has the favor of his parents. There is nothing he can do to change the fundamental nature of their love for him. Yet day by day, he can behave in ways that may increase or decrease how pleased they are with him. While his naughtiness or rebellion will not cause his parents to stop loving him, it may cause them to be disappointed in him or even to punish him. Meanwhile, his acts of love and his heartfelt obedience will not cause his parents to love him any more, but it may cause them to be more pleased with him and to feel greater pride in him. Their hearts will be glad when they see him living well and sorrowful when they see him living foolishly.

Because we relate to God as his children, we have the ability to please or displease him. While his love for us remains unchangeable, still we can behave in ways that are favorable or unfavorable. Favorable living seems to have been one of the concerns of the church in Thessalonica, which is why Paul explained to them how they could live lives that are pleasing to God (1 Thessalonians 4:1-12). They would please God as they practiced sexual purity, Christian community, and hard work. They would displease him if they fell into sexual sin, if they disrupted Christian community, or if they surrendered to lazy living. Part of Paul's ministry to every church was to instruct Christians in how they "ought to walk and to please God" (1 Thessalonians 4:1).

Jesus told his disciples they would prove their love through their obedience. "If you love me, you will keep my commandments" (John 14:15). God commands that we put sin to death and come alive to righteousness, that over the course of our lives we become increasingly conformed to the image of Jesus Christ (Romans 8:29). As our character comes to resemble Jesus' character, our actions begin to imitate Jesus' actions so that we begin to live not first for our own good but for the good of others. "In the same way, let your light shine before others, so that they may see your good works and give glory to your Father who is in heaven" (Matthew 5:16). This is the life that is pleasing to God, a life lived in conformity to the commands of God and to the glory of God. It is a life lived for the good of others.

Young Christian, is this the life you are growing into? Jesus Christ satisfied the wrath of God against your sin and drew you into a loving relationship with the Father. God loves you. He approves of you. And now he calls you to live a life that is pleasing to him, to live in such a way that you submit to him, that you bring glory to him. Join Paul in praying "that you may be filled with the knowledge of his will in all spiritual wisdom and understanding, so as to walk in a manner worthy of the Lord, fully pleasing to him: bearing fruit in every good work and increasing in the knowledge of God" (Colossians 1:9-10).

PURSUE THE FAVOR OF MAN

While the first priority of every Christian must be securing the favor of God, we also do well to pursue the favor of man. The two are often connected, as Solomon declared, "When a man's ways please the Lord, he makes even his enemies to be at peace with him" (Proverbs 16:7). In general, the kind of life that is pleasing to God is also pleasing to man. Paul aimed at this two-tiered approval as well, telling the church in Corinth, "we aim at what is honorable not only in the Lord's sight but also in the sight of man" (2 Corinthians 8:21).

Thus, it is no sin to want others to think well of us and to gain their approval. Of course, it is sin when others' approval becomes our ultimate desire, or when it leads us away from obedience to God. But when we seek God's approval first and then others', such a desire can actually be virtuous. "A good name is to be chosen rather than great riches, and favor is better than silver or gold," says Solomon (Proverbs 22:1). Paul goes so far as to explain that having a good reputation before unbelievers is a necessary qualification for a pastor: "Moreover, he must be well thought of by outsiders, so that he may not fall into disgrace, into a snare of the devil" (1 Timothy 3:7). We are to deliberately "give thought to do what is honorable in the sight of all" (Romans 12:17). Though unbelievers may not approve of your faith, they at least should not be able to doubt your sincerity or mock your hypocrisy.

While there is benefit in having the favor of all men, there is special benefit in having the favor of other Christians, and especially those of spiritual maturity. It is only believers who "have the mind of Christ" (1 Corinthians 2:16), who are equipped to evaluate us in light of God's word and to commend or reprove us according to its unfailing standard. For this reason, we need to participate in Christian community, where other Christians accept the responsibility to watch over us in Christian love, to teach us, encourage us, and even lovingly rebuke us. Their favor is our commendation.

Do you have friends, parents, pastors, or mentors who will encourage you and tell you how they see God's grace in your life? Will they also frankly call out any concerns they see? Find trusted people, invite them to speak into your life, listen patiently and without offense, prayerfully consider what they've said, then accept their assessment. Count their rebuke as God's grace in your life and count their favor as God's own approval.

CONCLUSION

As Jesus passed from childhood to adulthood, he advanced in submission, in wisdom, and in stature. As he advanced in all these ways in his teens and 20s, he gained the due reward:

divine favor and human favor. Both God and man observed his maturation and approved of his character and actions, for they were undeniable evidences of God's presence and God's blessing. He was living a perfect life, modeling the life God means for all of us to live.

Today, we hear of the importance of following our hearts, of being true to ourselves, of living according to our own standards. The Bible calls us to the exact opposite, to follow God's heart, to be true to him, and to live according to his standards. Self-approval is meaningless and deadly if it comes at the expense of God's approval. As you pass through your teens and 20s, you will have to choose again and again to pursue the favor of God and trust that as you pursue his favor, you will also gain the favor of people. As you advance in submission, wisdom, and stature, you can look forward to enjoying the favor of God and man.

STUDY GUIDE

1. *Who do you ultimately seek approval from?*

2. *Does your desire to please man trump your desire to please God?*

3. *How do you think your neighbors or unbelieving friends would react if you told them you were a Christian? Would they be surprised?*

4. *Do you live a double life?*

5. *Does your church community see you as an exemplary person? What evidence is there?*

6. *Have you found trustworthy to people to speak into your life to both encourage and rebuke you when they see fit?*

   • *If so, how do you respond when you receive rebuke?*

   • *Do you also speak life-giving encouragement and rebuke to other Christians?*

CHAPTER 6

Four Key Commitments

We have established that the one key pursuit for Christians in their teens and 20s is godly character. We have seen that this character is gained by submitting to authority and by pursuing wisdom, stature, and favor. As we conclude this little study, I want to offer four noble uses of this unique time in life. Your teens and 20s will not be wasted if you commit yourself to these pursuits.

A TIME OF SALVATION

Nothing is more important than ensuring you have experienced salvation, for there can be no true advances in character without it. Yet for many, especially those raised in Christian families, such confidence can prove surprisingly hard to come by. You may soon learn that a childhood profession of faith can seem very real in one moment and completely fake in another. While you hope and pray that your faith in Christ immediately overwhelms and eradicates all desire for sin, you inevitably find that you are torn between a longing to honor God and a longing to indulge in what God forbids. While you want to live confident in your profession, sometimes you waver and doubt.

The Bible teaches that salvation is a gift of grace that is given through faith. To be saved you must first acknowledge that you are a sinner who has offended a holy God, then acknowledge that Jesus Christ died on the cross as your substitute. But the faith you need to have is more than mere acknowledgment of this information; it is also a deep trust in God. You must trust that Jesus Christ has done everything necessary to save you from your sins and make you alive in him. What matters is not whether you can recall a moment of salvation at some point in the past, but whether today you are trusting in Christ. Have you put your faith in him? These years will be wasted unless you are a Christian. Make this a time of salvation.

A TIME OF SANCTIFICATION

Once you have put your faith in Jesus Christ and received his salvation, you are able to experience the joy of sanctification. Having been declared righteous, you begin to become holy. Some have described the Christian life as "a long obedience in the same direction," and that is exactly true. For the rest of your life you will be identifying sin and putting it to death while also recognizing righteousness and bringing it to life. The Christian life is composed of both of these—of putting off sin and putting on righteousness.

Your teens and 20s will be put to the best and highest use if you make them a time of sanctification. Even when you are a teen or young adult, you can make bold steps in identifying and overcoming sin and equally bold steps in embracing righteousness. In fact, during your teens and 20s, with the freedom of time and fewer responsibilities, you have more time and energy than ever to put sins to death now so that they won't plague you in later years. As a Christian you are indwelled by the Holy Spirit whose joy it is to motivate and empower this work and to join you in it. He operates primarily through the Word. It is in the Bible that you will learn what counts as sin and righteousness. It is in the Bible that you will best see the beauty of holiness. It is through the Bible that you will develop a longing to obey God who says, "You shall be holy, for I am holy" (1 Peter 1:16). Make this a time of sanctification.

A TIME OF PREPARATION

Your teens and 20s are also put to good use when they become a time of preparation. This booklet has been geared at helping you develop character that will last you for a lifetime. But that is only one kind of preparation. In these years, you can grow in other ways and as you do so, you will increase the ways God can use you in the days ahead. In your teens and 20s, you are preparing by storing up the resources that God will use in and through you for the rest of your life.

You can prepare by being diligent in your educational opportunities and continuing to accumulate knowledge. God can use every bit of knowledge you gain. You can prepare by learning new skills, whether they are related to vocation or hobbies or anything else. God can use every skill you have. You can prepare by learning Scripture and theology, listening carefully to every sermon every Sunday, being consistent in your personal devotions, and reading good books. God can use every bit of wisdom you have. The fact is, God cannot work with what you do not have, and these years are ideal for preparing yourself to be used by him. Make this a time of preparation.

A TIME OF ACTION

All throughout this booklet I have explained my desire that young Christians have a zeal to *be* before they have a zeal to *do*. The best use of these years is not to stack up accomplishments for God but to joyfully pursue God through godly character. Yet as I call for young Christians to focus more on character than accomplishment, I certainly do not wish to advocate apathy. This is not a call for low expectations, but for expectations that are rightly focused and properly prioritized. As a young Christian, you will have many opportunities to serve God by serving his people. Take them! Enjoy them! Make the most of them! Begin even now to use your gifts, talents, time, energy, and enthusiasm for the good of others and the glory of God. Aim at the great goal of giving glory to God by doing good for others. That is the very best way to live. Make this a time of action.

ADVANCE!

Thank you for reading to the end. It is my sincere hope that you have seen the importance of your teens and 20s as a time to advance. And it is my fervent prayer that you will use them first to advance in submission to God-given authorities, and to advance in those noble traits of wisdom, stature, and favor. May God be glorified in you and through you today and for the rest of your life. Always and forever, advance!

STUDY GUIDE

1. *Have you put your faith in Christ?*

2. *Are you prioritizing your sanctification? How much time do you spend in the Word on a regular basis?*

3. *How will you use your adolescence to prepare you for your life ahead?*

   - *What kind of skills will you seek to acquire?*

   - *Will you be diligent in learning as much as you can?*

4. *How will you use these unique years in your life to serve others?*

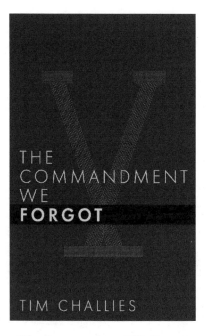

The Commandment We Forgot
Tim Challies

Set an Example
Tim Challies

The fifth commandment— "Honor your father and your mother"— is not just for children. Rather, it pertains to the whole of life and to every person of every age. In the home, the church, and the workplace, it provides a stable foundation for all of society. Yet we often neglect it and fail to appreciate its relevance to our lives. It is the commandment we forgot.

There are many ways to invest your time in your teens and 20's, but the Bible is clear: none is better than the pursuit of godliness. In Paul's letter to young Timothy, you (yes, you!) are called to be an example to your peers and even to older Christians. He calls you to set an example of maturity and godliness in your speech, conduct, love, faith, and purity.

Made in the USA
Lexington, KY
30 November 2019

57925986R00033